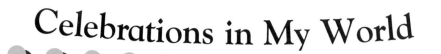

Celebrations in My World

100th Day of School

Reagan Miller

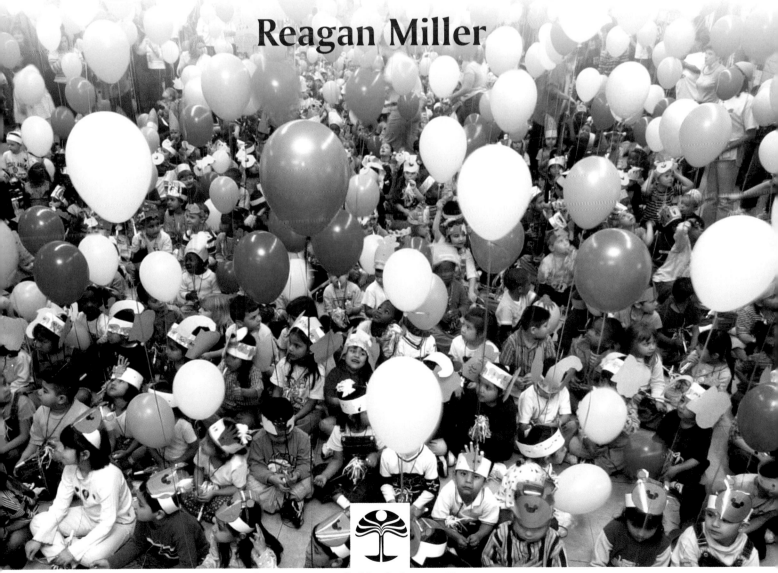

Crabtree Publishing Company

www.crabtreebooks.com

Crabtree Publishing Company
www.crabtreebooks.com

Author: Reagan Miller
Coordinating editor: Chester Fisher
Series editor: Susan LaBella
Editor: Adrianna Morganelli
Proofreader: Molly Aloian
Editorial director: Kathy Middleton
Production coordinator: Katherine Berti
Prepress technician: Katherine Berti
Project manager: Kumar Kunal (Q2AMEDIA)
Art direction: Cheena Yadav (Q2AMEDIA)
Cover design: Shruti Aggarwal (Q2AMEDIA)
Design: Shruti Aggarwal (Q2AMEDIA)
Photo research: Mariea Janet (Q2AMEDIA)

Photographs:
Associated Press: p. 1
Big Stock Photo: p. 12, 13; Cathy Yeulet: p. 30
Corbis: Noah K. Murray/Star Ledger: p. 27
Dreamstime: p. 11 (calendar); Sonya Etchison: p. 23; Hallgerd:
    p. 29; Natallia Khlapushyna: p. 20
Getty Images: Thomas Fricke: p. 9; Keystone/
    Hulton Archive: p. 17
Istockphoto: cover, p. 8; Ana Abejon: p. 5; Rhienna Cutler:
    p. 31; Bonnie Jacobs: p. 7
Masterfile: p. 4, 10, 15, 25
Photolibrary: Jeff Greenberg: p. 16; Jupiter Images:
    p. 18; Coll-Lisette Le Bon: p. 26; Scholastic Studio 10: p. 11
    (girl in classroom)
Shutterstock: p. 19, 22; Cheryl Casey: p. 14 (girl); Kentoh: p.
    28; Kynata: folio image; Natelle: p. 14 (inset bottom right);
    Dmitriy Shironosov: p. 6; Christophe Testi: p. 14
    (inset bottom left); Monkey Business Images: p. 24

Library and Archives Canada Cataloguing in Publication

Miller, Reagan
    100th day of school / Reagan Miller.

(Celebrations in my world)
Includes index.
ISBN 978-0-7787-4763-5 (bound).--ISBN 978-0-7787-4781-9 (pbk.)

    1. Hundredth day of school--Juvenile literature. I. Title.
II. Title: Hundredth day of school. III. Series: Celebrations
in my world

LB3533.M54 2009   j394.26   C2009-905260-1

Library of Congress Cataloging-in-Publication Data

Miller, Reagan.
    100th day of school / Reagan Miller.
       p. cm. -- (Celebrations in my world)
    Includes index.
    ISBN 978-0-7787-4781-9 (pbk. : alk. paper) -- ISBN 978-0-7787-4763-5
(reinforced library binding : alk. paper)
    1. Hundredth day of school--Juvenile literature. I. Title. II. Title: Hundredth
day of school. III. Series.

    LB3533.M55 2010
    394.26--dc22
                                                                    2009034879

Crabtree Publishing Company
www.crabtreebooks.com   1-800-387-7650

Printed in China/122009/CT20090915

Published in Canada
Crabtree Publishing
616 Welland Ave.
St. Catharines, ON
L2M 5V6

Published in the United States
Crabtree Publishing
350 Fifth Ave.
59th floor
New York, NY 10118

Published in the United Kingdom
Crabtree Publishing
Maritime House
Basin Road North, Hove
BN41 1WR

Published in Australia
Crabtree Publishing
386 Mt. Alexander Rd.
Ascot Vale (Melbourne)
VIC 3032

Contents

What Is the 100th Day of School?

The 100th Day of School is a special day **celebrated** at schools in many places around the world. It is a day to celebrate the first 100 days of the school year.

The 100th Day of School is a day for children to celebrate.

DID YOU KNOW?

The 100th Day of School is celebrated in schools across the United States, Canada, Ireland, England, and many other countries around the world.

Schools open on
different dates
in different places.

The 100th Day of School is not celebrated on the
same day by everyone. Different schools begin
classes on different dates so some schools
reach 100 days before others. Most schools
celebrate the 100th Day of School at the end
of January or in early February.

Who Celebrates?

The 100th Day of School is a holiday made just for kids! Adults do not celebrate this day—except for teachers. The 100th Day of School is celebrated in many preschool, kindergarten, and elementary schools.

You can wish your teacher and friends a "Happy 100th Day of School!"

Children who are taught at home may also celebrate this day. Unlike most other holidays, children go to school on the 100th Day of School. It is not a day off! We celebrate this day at school with our friends and teachers.

- The 100th Day of School is not a day off!

DID YOU KNOW?

The 100th Day of School is close to the halfway point in the school year.

7

Why Do People Celebrate?

In addition to celebrating the end of the first half of the school year, the 100th Day of School is also a day to celebrate the number 100. One hundred is an important number.

Some countries celebrate 100-year birthdays.

People celebrate the number 100 in different ways. For example, in the year 2000, we celebrated the end of a **century**. Countries and towns have big celebrations to mark their 100-year birthdays.

- This woman celebrates her 100th birthday.

DID YOU KNOW?

A person who lives to be 100 years old is called a centenarian. Do you know anyone who is a centenarian?

9

Calendar Countdown!

To celebrate the 100th Day of School you need to keep track of the number of school days that pass. Students begin counting on the very first day of school.

Most classrooms have calendars. Students use calendars to find the date of each day.

- On the first day of school, students start counting to the 100th day.

They can also use the calendar to count the number of days they have been in school. How do you keep track of school days in your classroom?

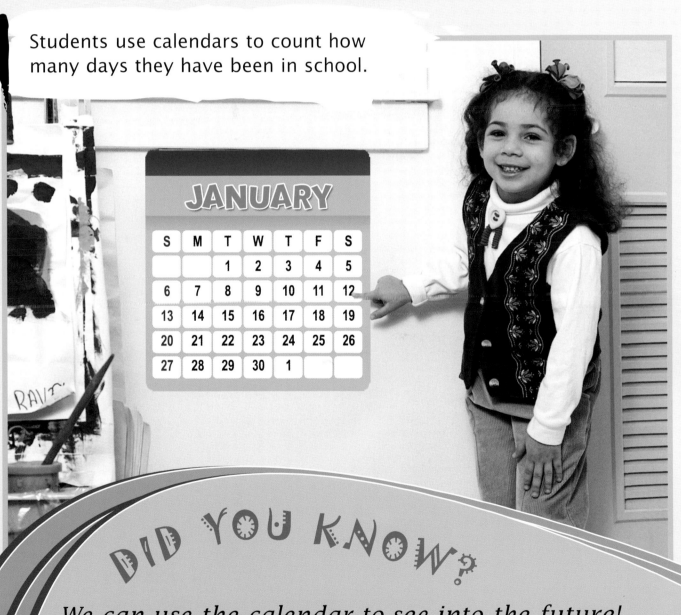

Students use calendars to count how many days they have been in school.

JANUARY						
S	M	T	W	T	F	S
		1	2	3	4	5
6	7	8	9	10	11	12
13	14	15	16	17	18	19
20	21	22	23	24	25	26
27	28	29	30	1		

DID YOU KNOW?

We can use the calendar to see into the future! Find today's date on a calendar. Then count 100 days. What will the date be in 100 days?

100 Days and Counting!

There are hundreds of ways to celebrate the 100th Day of School! Most schools celebrate with fun and interesting activities that use the number 100. Some activities may help children with counting. Children can practice counting to 100 in different ways.

- You can count by ones or by fives to 100.

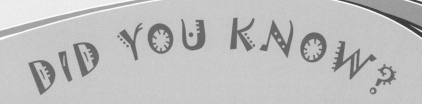

The number one followed by 100 zeros is called a googol. A googol is a very big number!

Sometimes, children use charts or other kinds of counters to count to 100.

They can count by ones. They can also skip-count by twos, fives, and tens. Children can use a hundred chart to help them skip-count. How many different ways can you count to 100? For an extra challenge, start at 100 and count down to reach number one!

13

Guessing Games

The 100th Day of School is a great time to practice **estimation**. Estimation is finding out about how much or how many. In some classrooms, teachers fill jars with objects, such as paper clips, marbles, or jellybeans.

The students look at the jars and estimate which jar has exactly 100 objects inside.

Which jar has 100 items?

Look at the bowl of candy below. Estimate whether it holds 100 candies. How would you check your estimate?

- Can you estimate the number of candies?

DID YOU KNOW?

You can estimate how long it takes to do something. Try estimating how much time it takes you to get to school in the morning.

Travel Back in Time

The 100th Day of School is a good time to learn what life was like 100 years ago. A lot has changed during the last 100 years.

Children went to a one-room schoolhouse 100 years ago.

DID YOU KNOW?

You can visit this Web site to find out what was happening 100 years ago from today: www.history.com/this-day-in-history.do

For example, 100 years ago many children went to school in a one-room schoolhouse. Students from all grades were taught together in the same room! Today, students use pencils and paper or computers to do their work. One hundred years ago, students used chalk and wrote on small chalkboards called **slates**.

Students wrote with chalk on slates 100 years ago.

17

100 Acts of Kindness!

The 100th Day of School is a happy day! In some classrooms, the children choose to share the happiness with others. Children bring in canned foods and put them in a large bin.

Children work together to bring in 100 cans of food to give to others.

DID YOU KNOW?

Share happiness anytime! Think of 100 kind acts you can do for others. Try to do one each day.

Children cover their hands with paint to make a "One Hundred Helping Hands" poster.

The goal is to collect 100 cans of food to give to a **food shelter**. In other classrooms, children cover their hands with paint. They place their handprints on a long piece of paper. This "One Hundred Helping Hands" poster reminds everyone to share happiness.

Around the World

Some schools use the 100th Day of School to learn how children in other parts of the world celebrate this day. Some teachers have their students write letters or send emails to schools in different parts of the world.

- A grade two class in Hawaii made puzzles with 100 pieces.

DID YOU KNOW?

You can say the number 100 in Spanish—ciento, or French—cent.

The students can make new friends and share their plans for their 100th Day of School celebrations. Students from one school in Texas sent letters to schools in Canada, the United States, Spain, and South Africa. They then found those places using a map of the world.

- A grade one class in Thorold, Ontario, celebrated by drawing pictures of how they would look when they are 100 years old!

21

Write On!

The 100th Day of School is a great day for students to let their imaginations run wild! There are many different creative writing ideas to celebrate this holiday.

Some students write about what they think the world will be like 100 years in the **future**.

- You can use your imagination to write about this holiday.

DID YOU KNOW?

Each year, children in the United States vote for their favorite books. The list has over 100 books. See it at www.cbcbooks.org/ readinglists/childrenschoices.aspx.

This boy enjoys a great 100th Day of School story.

In other classrooms, students may write about how they would spend 100 dollars. Some children draw pictures to go with their stories. Sometimes, students share their stories with their classmates.

23

Get Moving!

Games, sports, and activities are often a part of 100th Day of School celebrations. Children can get moving in many different ways. Try as many of these activities as you can! Count how many times you can jump rope in 100 seconds. You can dribble a ball 100 times or toss a beanbag with a friend 100 times.

• How many times can you jump in 100 seconds?

Grab a hula hoop and try to turn it around your waist 100 times. When you are finished, be sure to cheer 100 times!

• Be sure you drink a lot of water after you exercise.

DID YOU KNOW?

It is important to rest after doing exercises and drink a lot of water. Challenge yourself to sit still and not speak for 100 seconds! Can you do it?

A Date to Decorate!

These children helped make a chain of 100 paper dolls.

Making decorations and costumes is a fun part of any celebration. In some classrooms, students work together to make paper chains using 100 paper loops. They hang their chains in their classrooms. Some children decorate balloons to tie to desks and chairs in their classrooms.

Students can even wear special clothing to celebrate. At some schools, children make T-shirts or hats to wear on this holiday. They pin or glue 100 items to their T-shirts or hats, including buttons, stickers, pom-poms, and other items. Some kids also paint the number 100 on their faces!

These students made colorful hats to celebrate the 100th Day of School.

DID YOU KNOW?

The Roman numeral for 100 looks like this: C. You can use this symbol on your 100th Day of School decorations.

Hungry for Hundreds

The 100th Day of School is a busy day!
Children can get hungry after doing
so many activities. At some schools,
children make a special 100-piece snack.

The students and the teacher
bring in different food
items such as dried
fruit, seeds, and
chocolate chips.

- Raisins and dried
  fruits help make
  a tasty snack.

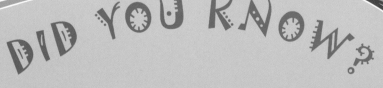

DID YOU KNOW?

*Make a snack that looks like 100. Cut a banana
in half for the one. Use two pineapple rings for
zeroes. What other foods can you use to make
the number 100?*

Students begin by washing their hands. They then work together to count out 100 of each item. Each group of 100 is put in a large bag.

The students shake up the bag to mix up the snack. Then, everyone can share the snack. What a yummy way to enjoy the 100th day!

● Shake the bag to mix up the snack.

29

Looking Back

The 100th Day of School is a perfect time for students to look back at all they have learned so far in the school year. It is a day to celebrate the happy **memories** made during the first 100 school days.

- Who have you met in your first 100 days of school?

DID YOU KNOW?

You can finish this sentence: On the first day of school, I could not _____, but on the 100th day of school, I can!

30

Celebrate all you have done in the first 100 days of school!

In some classrooms, each student takes a turn to share his or her favorite memory of the year. It is also a good time for students to set **goals** for the second half of the year. Students think about what they can do to make the second half of the year even better than the first!

31

Glossary

celebrate Observe with celebration and fun

century A period of 100 years

estimation The act of making a smart guess about how much or how many

food shelter A place that provides food and shelter for people in need

future A time yet to come

goal Something a person works hard at to achieve

memories Things you remember

slate A small tablet used to write on

Index